The Beach

Male and female masked crabs during courtship on the shore at night.

By the same author

The Field
Exploring the Woodland
Exploring the Hedgerow
Exploring the Park
Exploring the Seashore

The Beach

Written and photographed by

Leslie Jackman

The dunes. Rabbit tracks lead
right down to the tideline.

Evans Brothers Limited London

Published by Evans Brothers Limited
Montague House, Russell Square,
London, W.C.1.

First published 1974
Reprinted 1978

The photographs on pages 90 and 91
are by Rodger Jackman

Filmset in 12 on 13 pt Baskerville
and Printed Offset Litho by
Cox & Wyman Ltd, London, Fakenham and Reading

ISBN 0 237 44748 7   PRA 6112

Contents

Chapter One

The edge of the land

The sea wind swung the white bells of the sea campion and swept through the stiffer stalks of the sea thrift. Above the blackthorn hedge a herring gull hovered on the updraught and a blackbird screamed its alarm call over the cliff-top grass, disturbed by a wandering cat from the house over the hill.

There's a track that passes close against the hedge and it leads to a gap in the spiky thorns. As I passed through, the air was full of the scent of land plants.

Suddenly, there was the beach below and the salt sharp tang of the sea. Bright sand warm to the feet, the strong smell of seaweed and the roar of surf.

Left: Black-headed gull flying over the dunes.

Below: During the warm summer months the white flowers of sea campion bloom all over the cliffs.

Sea holly is a very distinctive plant with its prickly pointed leaves and powder blue flowers.

Seven oyster catchers curved in around the headland to land on the brightly coloured stones, wet with the sea. For a while the air was filled with their flute-like notes as they called to each other before settling to the more serious business of shell fishing.

I have known the beach for many years, yet every time I visit it there's something fresh to be seen. In autumn the migrant birds drop in – perhaps a shore lark or a phalarope; in winter an oiled guillemot or floating timber are brought in from the open ocean; in spring a host of creatures come inshore to lay their eggs; and in summer there is the possibility of a small octopus or jellyfish to add to the excitement.

There are old friends too. The pair of mallard that arrived eight years ago, the curlew that appears each January, the seven small turnstones and the pair of kestrels that each year nest on the cliff face.

Once or twice each year the north wind drops its blanket of snow and sometimes the sea mist billows in and a damp grey hush encircles the beach, but most often it's bright.

It is a small world easy to explore, bounded by two red sandstone headlands with the tall cliff behind and the sea billowing to the horizon.

Within these boundaries lies the beach I will tell you about. A wonderful place where so many exciting things wait to be discovered.

Top right: At the edge of the land lie the drifted plastic containers, some smeared with oil gathered in their journeys along the seaways.

Right: The beach in winter.

Top far right: Lesser black back gull sitting on eggs placed in a small depression near the top of the beach. These birds will 'dive bomb' any person walking too close to their nest.

Right: Hundreds of limpets lie along the tideline.

8

Chapter Two

The rocks

The rocks that spread across the middle of the beach are the home of many different kinds of shellfish.

The most obvious are the limpets with their pyramid-shaped shells clinging tightly to the rock surface where not even the biggest of waves can dislodge them.

At first glance they appear to be dull, sluggish creatures but I think you'd be surprised to know how active they can be.

When covered by the sea they come to life and move off in search of food. They crawl slowly using the large flat foot that previously held them to the rock and the head, with its two tentacles, sticks out in front rather in the manner of a tortoise.

As they move they swing from right to left, tongues rasping away at the tiny growths of seaweed that form their food. In the course of a few hours they may move many yards, but

Left: An edible sea urchin. This is the unfortunate creature caught by underwater divers and then dried out to make decorations and television lamps. How much more exciting the living creature is! In this photograph its long tube feet can be seen.

Below: A limpet beside the shallow mark left by another limpet after it died or was eaten by a herring gull.

finally they know the tide has turned and one by one the limpets return to the very same spot from which they started.

Nobody understands how they find their way back. There have been plenty of guesses but it is still a mystery and all we *do* know is that they always return to the same place.

Living for many years in one spot, and continually clamping down wears away a small hollow in the rock which can be seen after a limpet has died or been eaten by a gull.

In some zones the rocks are covered with bladder wrack and this is where the small flat periwinkles live, their green, yellow, red and black shells looking very much like the bladders of the seaweed. Perhaps this camouflage saves some of them from the oyster catchers, although I have often seen these little shells broken open. Maybe they were spotted by a hunting bird as they crawled along.

Most of the shells living among the rocks are univalves with coiled shells. The large foot on which they crawl is an ideal way of moving on such a surface and their powerful suction power saves them from being swept away by the surf.

One of the carnivorous shells which feeds on mussels and barnacles is the dog whelk. It has a most interesting way of feeding. It has a long ribbon-like tongue on which are a few sharp teeth and the whole thing is carried on the end of a kind of long snout called a proboscis. When it finds a suitable mussel shell or barnacle it settles down on it and begins to bore away with this ribbon of teeth. Using a slow rasping action the whelk makes a hollow and gradually a hole is rasped right through the shell of its prey. Then the ribbon tongue works something after the manner of a conveyor belt and carries the rasped-out food into the dog whelk's throat.

On the beach their shells vary from white to mauve and some have black and white stripes like rugger jerseys. It is said that the white shells tell you the dog whelk has been feeding largely on barnacles whereas the mauve-black or brown-pink ones have fed

on mussels. The stripes indicate a change of diet.

Every winter two men come down to the beach to collect winkles to sell for food. In the course of a single afternoon they may gather two sacks full, carrying them back up the cliff path on their backs. Since they do this several times each year it is surprising that there are still plenty of winkles left.

Left: Bladder wrack showing the large bladders that give it its name and keep it afloat.

Below: Puzzle. Find the dwarf periwinkles among the bladders of this bladder wrack.

Under the overhanging ledges of the inner reef, painted top shells live among the sponges and small cowries feed on the sea squirts.

There is one particular rock that is covered by mussels and thousands of them live here crowded together so tightly that there seems to be no room for them to grow. Each one is anchored to the rocks by a number of thin threads called byssus threads. These are squirted out by the mussel as a liquid which hardens in the water. The ends stick very firmly to the rock surface and in this way the mussel is held securely in place. Each thread is slightly elastic and this helps to reduce the force of the waves.

Shells, like the seaweeds, live in a particular part of the shore, each species being found in a fairly narrow band or zone.

The tiny, least periwinkle is found highest on the shore in what is known as the splash zone, which is wetted only by the highest of tides and spray from occasional waves.

On the other hand the painted top shell is found only on the lower part of the shore.

All the shellfish attract birds, for they are good to eat and seabirds like them – especially oyster catchers. There is a flock of seven that feed regularly on the beach and soon after they arrive the bay echoes with their flute-like calls. Their favourite prey is

into them. Quite early in life it settles out of the drifting plankton and drops down on to the rocks and begins to turn to and fro on one spot. Its shells have rasp-like ends and slowly they begin to wear away the rock, grain by grain.

There is no hurry and the piddock keeps up the action all day long, day after day, month after month until it has made a small tunnel into the rock. Now, of course, it is fairly safe from enemies. As it goes deeper it also grows larger, so the burrow goes further in and, at the same time, enlarges. Since the hole by which the piddock first entered the rock was tiny, the shellfish is now trapped

mussels which they crack open with sharp and powerful blows of their beak. An old fisherman I know calls them 'oyster crackers' and he reckons they eat many more shellfish than he does and he has been known to swallow fifty mussels at a meal! Perhaps over the year the birds do eat more than he does.

Then there are the herring gulls which will eat pretty well anything and they usually find something to their taste on the beach. They are lazy feeders and prefer the odd stranded shore crab or dead fish rather than having to deal with the more difficult task of opening shellfish.

Not all the shellfish live *on* the rocks. Some, like the piddock, prefer to bore deep down

Above left: Upper and lower views of a common starfish. This one has only four fully-grown arms and the fifth can be seen just beginning to grow. It was probably broken off due to some accident and starfish are able to re-grow damaged or lost arms.

Above: A painted top shell.

inside its 'cave'. Here it settles down to spend the rest of its life drawing in seawater and drifting pieces of food.

Piddocks have one further unusual habit. They give off a glowing light, the purpose of which is not known. So, deep in its burrow it continues to grow, surrounded by a ghostly light and safe for the many years it will live.

Eventually it will die and the large hole it has made is attacked by the waves' pressure. Slowly the hole enlarges and sometimes a few

small stones are thrown in by the sea to be whirled around and to wear away the rock further.

Much later perhaps, two or more piddock holes enlarge into each other and in the course of time the rock splits open.

This is one kind of erosion at work. It is a tiny part of the shaping of our coasts and in time past such erosion helped to carve out the soft rock and form the curving bay here at the beach.

Year after year the sea beats at the land and breaks away the base of the cliffs to cause great landslides to tumble down on to the sand below. Year after year the waves smash the massive boulders into large rocks and later, much later, the rocks are split into smaller stones which grind against each other, making each even smaller.

The seething sound that we hear as the waves break upon the shore is simply a mixture of water sounds and the rasping together of a million, million pebbles being rounded off into tiny grains of sand that form the place I call the beach.

Below: A piddock shell partly revealed when the rock that formed its burrow was broken in half.

On your beach

Search under rock ledges for sponges and sea squirts and various kinds of shellfish and starfish. By all means look at them closely *but be careful in handling them for many are delicate, and always return them to the place where they were found. Never remove* sea anemones, sponges or sea squirts and other fixed animals.

Make a map showing where the different kinds of seaweed grow.

If you count the number of barnacles in a ten centimetre square you can work out some idea of how many there are on a certain size piece of shore.

Look for the marks left by limpets.

If you have soft rocks in the area look for burrowing shellfish such as piddocks.

Make a collection of water-worn stones of different colours. If you varnish them with a clear varnish they will shine with all their full colours.

Chapter Three

The big rockpool

There is one rockpool that is a special favourite of mine. It's small, only about one cubic metre altogether.

It started life a thousand years ago when a limpet was knocked off the rock platform leaving its characteristic saucer-like depression behind. Through the years sea-driven sand rasped away at the little hollow and sun and frost flaked off pieces of rock.

As it grew larger, stones became lodged inside and these were whirled around by the surf to smooth and carve into the solid rock.

Left: The big pool.

Below: A group of anemones in a rock pool.

About the time of the Battle of Hastings this little pool was no larger than a tea cup and no living thing dwelt there. A few hundred years later when the Spanish Armada sailed past the beach the pool had increased to half its present size.

As the years rolled by it was shaped by countless waves and currents, until today it is almost round and some two metres across by half a metre deep.

It is still growing, of course, but to us humans it seems unchanged from year to year.

Twice each day the incoming tide sweeps into it, topping up the water that has

evaporated and cooling it suddenly after a sunny day. Occasionally the tide brings visitors from other parts of the shore, stranding them for a while among the regular inhabitants of the pool.

The pool is set among the glistening toothed fronds of saw wrack and bladder wrack. One plant of the latter has its holdfast (a sort of root) secured to the very rim of the pool, and the plant floats out over the surface buoyed up by its small floats and giving shade to that part of the pool.

On hot days much of the water evaporates and exposes a fringe of whitish-pink corallina, a tiny seaweed whose stems are in sections and coated with lime so that the plant is hard to the touch.

On the seaward side the edges of the pool are steep but the landward side has a deep undercut. I am always careful when I put my hand in there for it is just the sort of place a lobster might seek shelter.

There are two groups of animals in the pool. Those fixed animals such as sponges, sea squirts and sea anemones, and the visitors such as fish, crabs and prawns.

I often sit beside this pool and wait, keeping quite still so as not to warn the animals of my nearness. Let me tell you what happened one day when I dropped some pieces of fish into the pool.

A crab, half-buried in the sand, shrugged out of his hole and walked sidelong towards it, attracted no doubt by the scent. It very soon began to tear off small pieces and to lift them up to its scissor-like mouthparts.

Next to appear was a six centimetre long prawn dancing along on its delicate legs, the long feelers exploring before it. Soon it too was feeding.

Living in the pool at that time was a hermit crab and like others of his kind he had an old whelk shell as a home and on the pointed end of this shell lived a parasitic anemone.

The hermit quickly got to work on a piece of fish which he held with one claw whilst he picked pieces off it with the other, and passed them up to his mouth.

As so often happens, this hermit had a ragworm living with it in the whelk shell, curled around the centre column. Scenting the food, the ragworm put its head out of the shell and along the right 'cheek' of the crab. In this position the crab cannot touch the worm and the latter can obtain all the food it needs direct from its host's jaws.

Let me tell you the story of this strange partnership. One day a growing hermit crab takes possession of a large whelk shell and

Right: A hermit crab.

settles down in its new home. Some time later a ragworm comes crawling across the seabed and then very cautiously it crawls over the outside of the shell towards the front end. Waiting for just the right moment it suddenly glides inside the shell through a small gap that is always there on the right side of the crab.

The two live quite happily together. The hermit being an active predator catches plenty of food and this seems to suit the worm. In turn the worm keeps up a continual movement of its body and this helps to circulate the water inside the shell and so gets rid of the crab's waste products.

After a while there comes a time when the hermit wanders into an area where there are a number of anemones. They are called parasitic anemones and are sort of hitch-hikers waiting for a hermit crab to give them a lift.

As soon as a hermit comes within reach the anemone bends over and grips the shell with its tentacles, releases its sucker disc from the rock and loops it over to stick fast on to the shell. In less time than it takes to tell, the anemone is sitting comfortably on the whelk shell being carried to the next meal.

Its place in this partnership is not as a mere hitch-hiker but rather as a protector,

Above: Barnacles crowded together on the rock surface.

for those stinging tentacles armed with poison keep dogfish at bay. No fish will attempt to attack the crab whilst that anemone is sitting there.

At mealtimes the hermit feeds and the ragworm takes its share and, since the hermit is a rather untidy feeder, a great deal of scraps are left lying on the seabed.

Having fed, the hermit moves on and as it does so, the anemone bends over backwards with its tentacles spread across the sand and sweeps up the pieces that are left like a vacuum cleaner.

So a hermit crab, a ragworm and an

anemone all live together in an old whelk shell.

This relationship of three animals living together is called commensalism or sharing the same table. Although called a *parasitic* anemone it is not in fact a parasite in the normal sense of the word because it helps its host to the extent that it protects it from enemies.

One final note. Most anemones close quite slowly when food touches them, but this parasitic anemone grips food instantly and smothers it with its tentacles in less than three seconds. Perhaps this is because it has to seize food quickly since the hermit moves off in quite a hurry at times.

If you enjoy those long Latin names that roll off the tongue, try *Calliactis parasitica*, that's the anemone; *Eupagurus bernhardus*, that's the hermit crab; *Nereis diversicolor* is the ragworm.

To return to my pool watching. Around the pool on the smooth rock surfaces hundreds of barnacles are attached, each only a few millimetres high and shaped like miniature volcanoes.

Barnacles are related to crabs but have adopted a fixed way of life and through the ages have developed protective plates that cover their bodies and cement them to the rocks.

By watching very closely I can see them open and from the small hole in the top a sweep net curves out through the water and returns inside. This action is repeated every two seconds. The net is shaped rather like a hand with the fingers slightly bent around, and its purpose is simply to catch drifting particles of food. Furthermore, this food-catching device is actually made up of what would be the normal walking legs of their relatives, so in one way it can be said that barnacles feed by kicking their food into their mouths!

Darwin, the great naturalist, wrote a very long and detailed paper on barnacles and he believed that his studies of this small creature helped to give him some of the basic

Left: In summer months sea hares, a kind of sea slug, come into the beach to lay their eggs. They feed on a green cellophane-like seaweed called sea lettuce.

Below: Blennies.

background that he needed to make so many remarkable discoveries.

Living in their protective shells they are safe from many predators, but wrasse and blennies both feed on them. These two species of fish have strong teeth that can crush the shells and their tough stomachs can also manage the sharp fragments.

On some of the stones lying on the bottom of this pool live large numbers of tube worms. Each lives within the white limestone case it has built and they are shaped rather like very elongated ice-cream cones.

Under a hot summer sun the colours of the pool are bright but I have seen it in mid-winter with a film of ice over the surface and snow-rimmed.

Throughout the years it will support a number of regular inhabitants such as barnacles, limpets and the seaweeds. Occasional visitors will arrive such as sea slugs or a drifting jellyfish or a flatfish and a shoal of tiny mullet.

This is the great fascination of the pool – there is always something new to be seen in its clear depths.

On your beach
Take a small piece of fish and feed some of the creatures in the rockpool. If you place it on the bottom they will come out to feed, but be patient and wait awhile, it will not all happen at once.

Visit a number of pools and search under the seaweed curtains for shellfish, crabs and starfish and sponges.

If you find a hermit crab tip the shell over very gently and then watch the crab right itself and walk away.

If you find a starfish, place it out on the sand in the pool, or on a rock and watch it move along. If you pick it up carefully you will be able to see its tube feet in motion.

Remember that starfish do not sting although many people think they do.

Chapter Four

Seaweed jungle

There is a part of the beach where the giant laminaria grow that is like an underwater jungle in miniature.

These great seaweeds stretch upwards towards the surface swaying to and fro as the wave's swell passes by. On a sunny day their fronds cast moving shadows down to the seabed, blue-black and eel-like over the silver sand.

A corner of the beach where sea belt grows thickly. Its long fronds are sometimes dried and hung in the house as a weather forecaster. The frond goes crisp for dry weather and limp and damp for wet weather.

Like the trees in a forest there are many different kinds and the largest are the thick, rubbery oarweeds or cows tails. They are perennials, that is they grow for a number of years and each year as the fresh growth starts, the old fronds are cast off and washed ashore on the tideline.

Tangle is another kind. It has a thick stem up to one and a half metres in length, one end divided into many tiny pieces which form its holdfast. The upper end spreads like the fingers of a vast hand with ten or more flat fingers nearly two metres in length.

A few years ago there was the lowest tide for seventy years on the beach and on that

occasion it was possible to wade among these seaweeds. Unsupported by the sea they were still firm enough to stand upright, and as I waded among them they reached up to my waist.

One of the best known of these huge seaweeds is sea belt. It has frilled fronds up to one and a half metres long and fifteen centimetres in width. Dried and hung up it can be used as a weather forecaster – the fronds becoming hard in dry weather and softening on the approach of rain.

The largest of all is furbelows. It stretches out for four metres or more and can be as wide as three metres. A single plant may weigh nearly fifty kilogrammes, yet it is only an annual and grows to this enormous size in a single season.

Much more delicate is the dabberlocks which looks its best in the warm days of summer.

Many of these laminaria provide a home for a variety of sea creatures which find protection within the branching roots of the holdfast. Two or three ragworms, six or seven

Below: Furbelows, one of the largest laminaria which sometimes grows up to four metres in length and nearly as much in width.

Bottom: Tangle growing amongst sea belt.

shells, sponges and a group of sea squirts may inhabit a single holdfast.

Their stems or stipes are often coated with hydroids and the older plants of cuvie, another kind of laminaria, have a red seaweed growing on their stems.

It is in this seaweed jungle that dogfish lay their eggs among the holdfasts, anchored by their long threads.

Below: Dog whelks and their egg capsules among mussels and barnacles.

Bottom: Sea thongs.

Sometimes on a quiet summers' afternoon a shoal of spotted gobies swims between the swaying fronds. In July and August the mullet bask with their backs occasionally breaking surface and in September a school of bass hunt among the stems for fat prawns. Cormorants dive and swim through the avenues of this seaweed searching for the fish that live there or are simply passing through.

Normally it is quiet down there, but when the storm winds blow, the white-capped rollers crash through this jungle and then the great seaweeds are torn free and cast up high on the beach.

In sun, rain and wind they quickly rot and as they break up the minerals they took from the sea to help them grow are released back into the water. Thus the death of a plant enables others to grow and although under winter skies there are many big gaps in the jungle, next summer will see them filled in and the mullet will bask once more.

On your beach
Try to find a good sized piece of sea belt. Take it home and hang it up in a shed, greenhouse, conservatory or porch and see if it forecasts the weatherp

Look carefully among the twisted holdfasts of some stranded laminaria. Seashells often live there.

Some of the smaller stranded seaweeds can be made into a collection. Arrange the fronds attractively on a piece of newspaper and place another few thicknesses on top with a book to weigh it down. Change the papers each day until the specimen is really dry and then stick it lightly into an exercise book and label it. If you leave the specimen between the same sheets of paper for too long it will stick fast and you will not be able to detach it for mounting.

Chapter Five

Birth of a dogfish

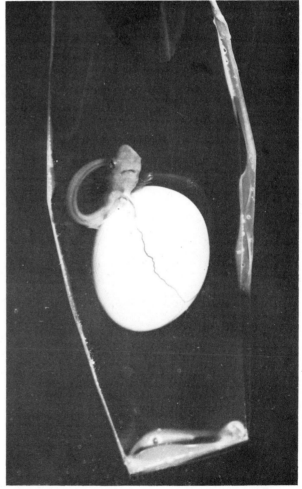

Mermaid's purse. This is the capsule laid by the female dog-fish and the threads with which she secures it to seaweed can be seen. Inside the semi-opaque case life is beginning although at present only the yolk can be seen.

One month old. In four short weeks the tiny life spot has grown into a small fish . . . still only five millimetres in length.

It is called a mermaid's purse. The gold it contains is the coloured yolk of an egg and the purse strings the thin threads which anchor it to the seaweed. It is between seven and ten centimetres in length and about three centimetres in width. It is the egg capsule of a dogfish.

A few days ago the female fish swam in to the bay and laid the egg. Then she took the long tendrils in her mouth and swam round and round and in and out of the seaweed twining the threads amongst the holdfasts until the egg capsule was securely anchored and safe for the five to seven months it would take to hatch.

Inside the capsule was a large yolk sac nearly as large as the yellow part of a hen's egg. When it is first laid this yolk has a tiny microscopic life spot on it which is the very beginning of the baby fish.

A month later the youngster is a centimetre long but little thicker than a piece of thread. From the centre of its stomach a thin red blood vessel goes out to branch into a network that surrounds the yolk. The stored food in the yolk sac passes into these tiny blood vessels and is carried along to the fish's body. As the baby fish grows the yolk becomes steadily smaller.

I have often watched through the

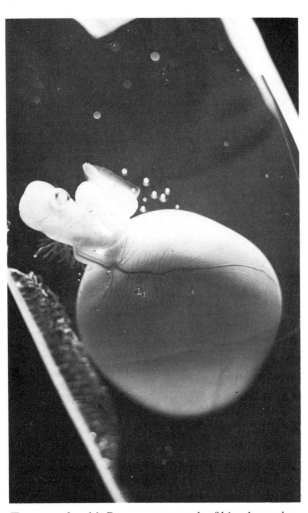

Two months old. By now a network of blood vessels is spreading across the yolk to take food into the growing body of the baby dogfish.

Three months old. Now about two centimetres in length, the little dogfish still has external gills which extend from each side of its head. It constantly moves by flexing its tail.

months as one of these small dogfish grows and it is a wonderful feeling to be aware of this tiny speck of life swaying in the currents.

Each time I return to the shore I marvel that it is still there, especially after one of the great storms. Each time I look it has grown a little more until finally comes the day when I find the capsule is empty. Having fed for seven months, protected by the walls of the mermaid's purse the little dogfish has finally swum free.

I look out to sea knowing that somewhere out there is a little fish no longer protected but now alone and part of the web of life in the sea. Perhaps eating, perhaps being eaten, for life in the sea can only survive by that simple food chain.

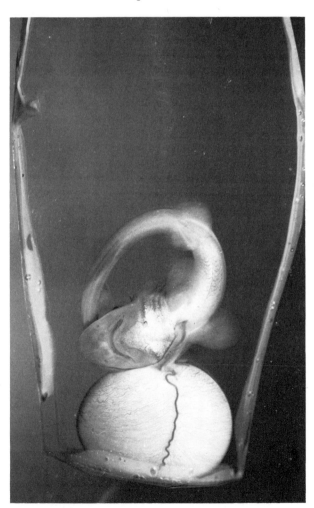

Age five months. The feathery external gills have been reabsorbed and it now breathes through normal gills. Seawater for breathing is drawn in through a small hole in the end of the egg capsule.

A few weeks later and the yolk sac has nearly been fully absorbed and the young fish is practically ready to emerge from its egg and swim into the open sea. For a few days the remaining yolk will serve to feed it.

Chapter Six

Rollers Reef

A little way out to sea some rocks rise out of the water like the back of a stranded whale. This is Rollers Reef. People cannot reach it except by boat so it is seldom disturbed by humans and in consequence it is a great place for seabirds. From time to time they go there to rest and preen after feeding or to roost during the hours of darkness.

The most common are the herring gulls and any time I land there I find signs of their feeding. Like birds of prey, these gulls eject the indigestible parts of their food in the form of a pellet. At first the pellets are held loosely together but as they dry they break up and then the bones and scales and hard body parts of the food the gull has eaten can be seen.

Some of the birds that rest on Rollers Reef follow the trawlers for food, flying astern and diving down to pick up the pieces thrown overboard as the crew gut the fish. Each boat returning to harbour has its own flock of herring gulls and although they are always there when the catch is being sorted out one

Left: A herring gull on the alert as it flies past.

Right: The pellet of a herring gull.

Far right: In this photograph the bones from the pellet have been set out in order to try and identify the fish. It appears to be a small fish such as a whiting, probably picked up by the gull in the fish market or by following a trawler.

never sees them whilst the boat is trawling its nets along. I guess the birds understand that there is no food for them until the catch is hauled aboard.

Another gathering of herring gulls sit around and wait for the arrival of the town dust carts at the local dump.

When one arrives, it backs up to the edge of the tip and begins to dump its load of rubbish. Immediately there is a swooping white cloud going on to the dust cart as a thousand herring gulls begin to pick up the scraps.

When you think about it, its a strange place to find seabirds. Here amongst the cornflake

His waste products provide an abundance of food and the population of herring gulls has grown as an almost direct consequence. If these same gulls had to feed on the natural foods that the beach provided they would be unable to find enough and very soon their numbers would decline.

Local residents get very upset about the gulls and blame them for making a great deal of mess around the dump area. This is a pity because in fact the birds are doing a most useful job of work. They are simply eating bits of food that might otherwise attract rats, and given a choice between rats and herring gulls I know which I prefer.

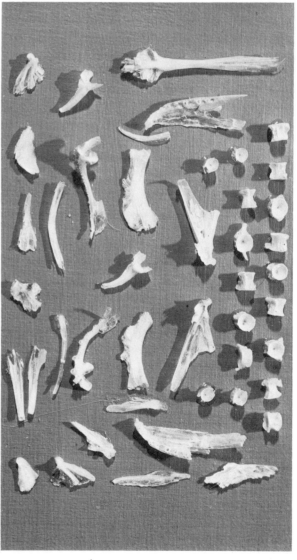

packets, detergent containers and the polythene is not the perfect habitat for herring gulls, yet among all this rubbish there is the waste from the hotel kitchens.

The man in charge of the dump told me an interesting fact about what goes on here. Apparently the gulls arrive during the late afternoon when the carts bring in the refuse from the hotels. During the morning the carts are visiting private houses and the crafty birds have learned that the real pickings come from the hotels – so that's when they come to feed.

The trawlers and the rubbish dump are two examples of how the life of a particular species has been affected by the activities of Man.

I am also quite certain that if they were rare birds we would all be queueing up to watch them.

As the population of herring gulls grows, the nesting sites on the cliffs and offshore rocks become too crowded and the birds have to spread out into new areas. These are not easy to find for Man has taken most of them over and built promenades below the cliffs. So the unfortunate gulls take the next best place which happens to be the rooftops of houses in the fishing villages and tourist resorts.

A fisherman friend of mine spends many hours each summer fishing for mackerel out in the bay and he knows one particular herring gull that always flies out to join him. Usually it sits on his bows and as it has been doing this for some years the two of them have become friends.

If he has a good evening's fishing he usually offers the bird a fish. He told me that one evening he offered it four small mackerel (we call them joeys locally) which it swallowed one after the other. When it tried to take off it was too heavy to become airborne and simply 'crashed' on to the sea surface!

Some of the local herring gull population have learned that there is plenty of food at the duck pond in the park, where a large

number of mallard ducks grow fat on pieces of bread. The gulls dive bomb the ducks and try to terrify them off the food.

Out on the reef there are also black-headed gulls. They are delightful birds with such elegant flight and delicate ways of feeding. They sweep in out of a great circle, brake with their wings and hover lightly before dipping to pick up the food. Then immediately they are off again cutting bright arcs against the sky.

When the sea is rough they hover over the breakers or skim the foaming crests to pick up morsels too small to be seen by the human eye.

In winter they have white heads with a small dark spot by the eye, but with the coming of spring their chocolate-coloured hoods begin to grow over their heads and in the bright light these look black and hence give the birds their name.

Each day three cormorants come to Rollers Reef to dry out. It is most important to a diving bird to keep its plumage in perfect condition so the cormorants sit on the highest rocks with their wings stretched out to dry in the sun and breeze.

Not far from the beach there is a lake and at its edge is an old beech tree on which cormorants have long rested. They sit there turning from side to side to catch every breeze and at the same time they preen all over their

Above: The beauty of flying black headed gulls.

Top: Herring gull picking up pieces of food from surface of water.

Left: A fish market orator. Herring gulls are so used to man that they appear to have lost all fear of him.

31

body by a snake-like movement of the long neck.

The tree has been killed by their droppings and now stands like a whitened skeleton with as many as twelve cormorants festooned on its branches.

Over the years Rollers Reef has had a few unusual visitors. An Atlantic or grey seal used to haul out there at low tide every day for nearly a month but quite suddenly it had gone. After one great storm I saw a great skua take off and fly northwards to more familiar grounds.

And one bright day as I watched the reef there was a sudden flash of rainbow and a kingfisher flew by.

Today, as I write, it is very quiet beside the sea but I can plainly hear the gentle lapping of the calm waters against the edge of Rollers Reef and the mirror surface of the sea reflects the gulls as they fly by.

Maybe if I sit here a little longer I'll see a porpoise break surface or a garfish leap from a shoal of summer mackerel. After all there is always something happening around here.

Gull watching

If you are prepared to have a little patience then watching seabirds can be great fun. A pair of binoculars will help but as these are rather expensive you may have to try and borrow a pair from Dad or an uncle. They are not essential though and plenty of action can be spotted by going to any place where you know seabirds gather.

The secret of watching is to concentrate on one bird and follow it as it walks, flies or swims around. In flight try to follow one as it swoops and soars over the waves and you will find each bird tends to have a sort of beat or flight path which it follows time and time again.

Use a good reference book to try and identify some of the birds you are watching. Your local library probably has a selection so why not ask the librarian?

Search for gull pellets but be prepared for a long look for they are not easy to discover.

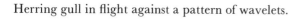

Herring gull in flight against a pattern of wavelets.

DIARY

March 10th

A really warm spring day so I went along to watch the fishermen making pots from twisted withies. They leave them out on the ground in rows and often there is enough sap in the stems to cause the leaves to sprout so the pot appears to be actually growing.

Up on the quay the seines were out and being repaired after their long winter storage. With the modern use of brightly coloured synthetic fibres the nets are quite colourful and silver plastic floats have replaced the old natural corks.

Below: Making crab pots from twisted withies, among the reeds.

One fisherman had left a pile of whelk pots out and this group was made with wire and ropes twisted around instead of using the withies that are used for lobster and crab pots.

Below left: Nets on the quayside.

Below right: Boat loaded with net which has round stones from the beach as weights.

Right: A wave breaking on the shore.

Below: A large hermit crab in the shell of a Whelk. This one has two parasitic anemones on the shell.

March 15th

Another warm day so I went down to the beach. A few lazy waves were breaking on the shore and it was possible to look right through them.

This made me decide to take a look in the big pool. First discovery was a hermit crab which must have wandered in from deeper water because it was really very large.

Searching among the seaweed I found a small spider crab known as macropodia. It was about seven centimetres from claw-tip to claw-tip and the body the size of a large pea.

Under one large ledge was the tip of

Above: A common spider crab, partly eaten by gulls.

Left: Macropodia, a small spider crab with a body the size of a pea.

a red claw, it was a large spider crab. Now I have seen these often in crab pots, but they are most rare on the shore and this makes me wonder. The hermit crab, the macropodia and the large spider crab are all normally found in deep water so what coincidence has brought them together in the big pool on this day in early spring? There has been no storm to wash them in.

One possibility does occur to me and that is that the fishermen put their pots out here in the bay and maybe they were clearing one out as the boat came close in, but even that is a very small chance.

Many green shore crabs in all the pools and under rocks. I was most careful to replace the rocks after searching under them because each one shelters a large number of species and they do need a roof over their heads to protect them from sunlight, wind and rain.

Walking back across the sandy beach I saw a small sand crab.

Left: Rocky shores like this are ideal hunting grounds.

March 28th

The sea slugs have arrived. They are late this year. Found about twenty of them and plenty of signs of their egg ribbons attached to the rocks. Some of the eggs had hatched so the slugs must have been here for some time.

Blennies plentiful everywhere.

Above: Blennies are always on the look-out.

Left: A close-up look at a green shore crab, reveals its mouth and stalked eyes.

May 29th

Out on the dunes I found a number of
oyster catcher nests – well hardly nests,
but rather small hollows in the grassy cover
among the stones and sand containing two
or three eggs.

I climbed up a high dune and lay down
in the marram grass and with my binoculars
looked around to see signs of birds. I spotted
one oyster catcher sitting on her eggs, but
by the time I drew near she had run off.

In a pile of rusty barbed wire, built into
the rim of a very rusty and ancient milk
churn was the nest of a carrion crow, built
of marram stems and lined with sheep's

wool. There are plenty of sheep here on the dunes so there is no difficulty in finding nesting material. The young crows opened up their beaks as I approached probably thinking it was the parent returning with food.

The black-headed gull colony was pretty lively and there were baby chicks everywhere.

Far left top: Black head gull chicks and two unhatched eggs.

Far left bottom: Sitting tight among the stones, an oyster catcher incubates her eggs.

Below left: Arcs cut by marram grass as it twists in the sea wind.

Below right: Newly hatched black headed gulls.

Bottom: Two carrion crow chicks open their mouths, whilst a third sleeps in their nest.

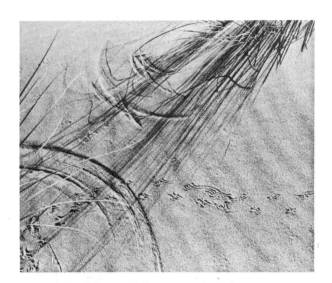

May 30th

This is the time of year on the shore when I can never be quite certain whether it is spring or summer, but in general I reckon summer begins on June 1st. After all, seasons come slowly and blend into each other out of doors so a particular date is unimportant I suppose.

Below: Cliffside flowers in June.

June 10th

The cliffs are a riot of colour with all those lovely flowers we know so well. Today the sun was hot with a sea wind sending updraughts over the cliffs and the white flowers of sea campion were rustling to and fro on their short stems.

All over the cliff face were patches of pink sea thrift or sea pink and some of the herring gulls had their nests among the clumps. What fortunate birds to have so lovely a nesting place and what a contrast from the carrion crow's nest in the barbed wire. Bright yellow kidney vetch grew amongst the grass.

A few blue and mauve blossoms of vipers bugloss added their colour to the scene, although these tend to grow on the shingly part of the beach rather than on the cliffs.

Right: Vipers bugloss growing on the shore.

Below: Sea pinks can be found growing all along the cliffs.

Bottom left: Wild carrot has white flowers with a reddish centre.

Bottom right: Rock samphire finds a roothold, just above the highest tides.

June 18th

This is the time of year when the seaweeds look their best for the new growth is still relatively undamaged by surf. I tried to imagine easy ways of remembering the names of some of these seaweeds and decided that bladder wrack was easy – after all one has only to remember the bladders. Saw wrack is another good one because the edge of the frond is toothed like a saw, hence saw wrack, toothed wrack or serrated wrack; three names for the same plant. I suppose knotted wrack looks a little like a piece of knotted string but as for dabberlocks I would think its Latin name

makes more sense. It is called *Alaria esculenta* and it certainly is eaten in parts of this country where it grows.

Left: Dabberlocks.

Bottom left: The bladders of bladder wrack are filled with gas which keeps it buoyant.

Below: Dahlia anemone. The white central disc is its mouth.

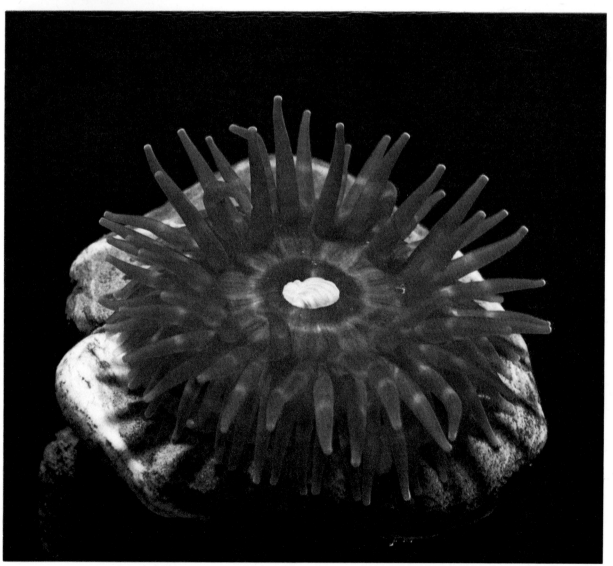

June 26th

Down to the beach for the midnight lowtide. Took the lamp and started looking for the dahlia anemones which, after dark, open fully out and are quite flower-like. Saw one as big across as a tea plate. There were red ones, pink ones and some colourful striped ones and all of them were to be found along the underside of rock overhangs and in small crevices. I touched some and their tentacles felt quite sticky. In fact, of course, this is due to hundreds of tiny stinging cells being discharged into the skin each one attached to the anemone by a microscopic thread, hence the sticky feel.

Some of the pools had fine snakelocks anemones in them but most of these were closed up. They tend to do this at night. They like bright sunny pools because they have cells of an algae in their tentacles and these need sunlight for the chlorophyll they contain.

A few shells were lying on the surface and one beautiful rayed trough shell had absolutely perfect rays on it.

Masked crabs were everywhere. It is amazing how these crabs can only be seen at night. If I visit the shore in daylight I never see a single one. As soon as the light from my lamp shone on to them they commenced to burrow down for cover.

Saw a great many starfish. This is another species which can be seen more frequently at night for it is then that they come out from under the seaweed and crawl out of hidden crevices. On the sandy beach the burrowing starfish were on the top of the sand and over on the rocks the common starfish were plentiful.

Picked up one specimen of a brittlestar nearly eighteen centimetres across – that's some brittlestar!

Below: Snakelocks anemone in daylight. By night the tentacles tend to droop.

Bottom: Rayed trough shell. A sand-burrowing bivalve.

Right: Burrowing starfish, on the beach at night.

Far right: Common starfish clinging to rocks.

Bottom right: Female masked crab. These crabs walk about after dark, and leave their tracks on the beach.

Left: Sea bindweed.

Below: A close-up look at a brittlestar reveals its complicated structure.

Top right: The restharrow grows very low against the shingle of the beach.

Bottom right: Shoals of mullet often come inshore during the summer months.

July 1st

Went down to see if there were any mullet about and on the way back noted that restharrow and sea bindweed are now in flower in the shingle at the top of the beach.

This sea bindweed is a very low growing plant and quite small whereas its relative that grows in the hedges will often reach a height of three to four metres. But there is no hope for a plant to grow to that height on the beach, it is too harsh an environment.

July 19th

The water in the rockpools is quite hot and much of it has evaporated because I saw a rim of salt along the waterline. This means that seashore creatures living in rockpools must be able to stand quite sudden changes of water density and salinity and also changes in temperature. I imagine that when the tide returns and floods these pools there is a sudden drop in temperature of as much as twenty degrees.

August 2nd

A wet, miserable sea mist came in and covered the sun. I saw it rolling up over the sea wall like a huge smoke-screen.

August 20th

Where the dunes meet the beach a number of plants of sea rocket are in bloom. One was actually growing on the seaward side of the drift line and most of them had tangles of seaweed around their lower stems.

Lyme grass is looking its best now and also the sea plantain.

Left: Lyme grass growing on the edge of the beach.

Below: A rocky corner of the beach.

September 3rd

Sometimes in the autumn and winter when it is very quiet, guillemots rest on the rocks. So it was today, and I was able to get very close to the bird by simply moving in slowly. For a few moments we looked at each other, less than two metres apart, and then the guillemot waddled into the sea, dived and so disappeared. In the springtime they nest on narrow shelves on the cliffs at Berry Head but in recent years their numbers have declined due to the disastrous effects of pollution.

September 12th

Fed the swans that fly in to the beach from a distant duck pond. They come here to browse among the seaweed at the edge of the sea.

Below: Two mute swans, visitors from a nearby park, feed at the edge of the sea.

Left: Guillemot. This bird catches fish by diving and swimming underwater.

September 22nd

It is amazing how very delicate objects are sometimes washed ashore undamaged. I found a test of a sea urchin and looked at it with a hand lens. How beautifully it is made and what a great deal of tiny detail there is in this shell of a sea urchin. They are collected locally and left to dry in the sun to make containers for lights and that seems to me to be about the most unthinking thing one could do to such pretty creatures.

Alive, the edible sea urchin is a delicate shade of purple and surrounded with thin, waving tube feet and the largest may measure up to the size of a grapefruit.

The edible urchin tends to be found in much deeper water than the purple tipped sea urchin which is common under rocks on the shore.

September 29th

Stranded among the seaweed was a mermaid's purse but it was empty and the little skate had emerged. These tiny fish when first out of the egg case are less than four centimetres across and most of them hatch during the warmer summer months. The cases get washed ashore with the first rough seas.

The name mermaid's purse is also used to describe the egg capsule of the dogfish. The photograph shows a baby dogfish with its yolk sac.

Left: Young skate.

Far left: An edible sea urchin with its hundreds of tube feet slightly extended.

Below: The developing dogfish embryo slowly absorbs the yolk of its egg, to which it is attached, whilst it breathes through feathery gills.

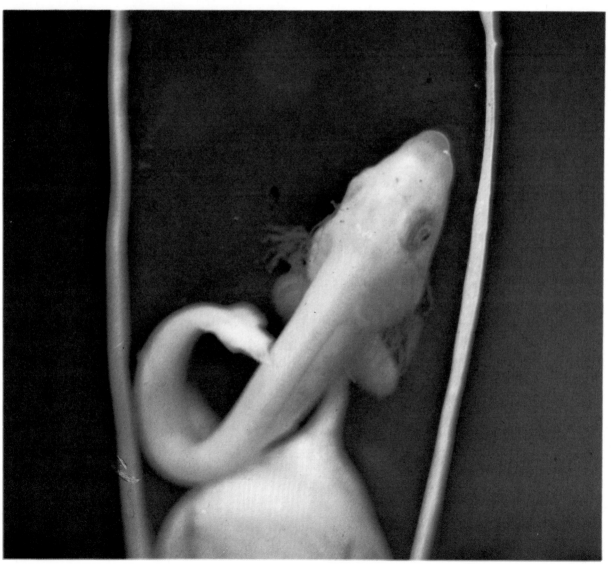

September 30th

This is the best time of the year to take
a look at the dunes because there are fewer
people about. Hedgehogs are still active
because I found their tracks among the
rabbits'.

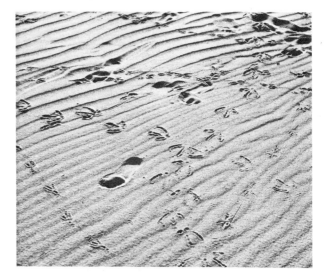

Top right: Tracks among the wave-like patterns
made by the wind.

Right: Tracks show where a rabbit wandered
across the track of a herring gull, the latter easy
to identify because of the size of the webbed foot.

Below: Limpets on the shore-line.

Far right top: A small stone covered with the
limestone tubes of the keeled tubeworm.

Far right bottom: Rabbits tracks in the snow on
the cliff top.

October 14th

During the night a blizzard came out of the north-east. Down on the shore a rock-pool was covered with a thin film of ice and the sand buried under a foot of snow.

The wind had caused a rough sea to wash ashore a host of shells but it was three days later – October 17th – that I found them.

A piece of red sandstone rock was completely covered with the white tubes of the keeled tubeworm and must have been washed in from the outer reef.

October 19th

For three days it has been blowing from the east, and now the beach is littered with flotsam and jetsam and the Plastic Tideline is there for all to see. Why do we use the sea as a dump? We are still doing it, for today I have read in my paper that a disused chemical factory in Eindhoven has become dangerously infected with weed killer. So they are going to demolish it and take the entire remains by barges and dump them into the Atlantic, 360 miles off Cape Finisterre, Spain. This is the sort of muddled thinking that leads to future problems. That filth can do no good on the seabed,

and one day tides and currents will bring it ashore to foul some beach.

On one part of the beach a group of red-nose cockles were wide open and many of them had been eaten by passing herring gulls. Oyster catchers had been having a field day with some mussels which they had opened using a powerful beak blow upon the part of the shell directly over the muscle that keeps the shell closed. In this way the mussel is unable to keep closed and so the bird gets its meal.

Top left: Flotsam and jetsam . . . better called plain rubbish . . . on the tideline.

Bottom left: After the gale. Stranded rayed trough shell, red-nose cockles, carpet shell and many others lie dying on the strand-line.

Below: Collected mussel shells that have been opened by oyster catchers.

Bottom: The vari-coloured shells of the flat periwinkle.

Shellfish of all kinds are lying on the beach. The thin pink shells of thin tellins, cockles, queens and rayed trough shells and the vari-coloured flat periwinkles carpet the shore with colour.

Plenty of sea mice lie among the seaweed. They all seem to be dead and no doubt the mauling they must have suffered in the surf soon killed these rather delicate worms that normally live beneath the muddy sand in quieter surroundings.

A huge log was stranded so I took a closer look and discovered that it was riddled with the burrowings of the teredo. I wonder how long it had been in the sea and from what far place it had come?

Below: Thin tellins are the most delicate shell found on the shore.

Bottom: The sea mouse, a very large marine worm.

Top right: Sea life stranded after the storm.

Bottom right: A dead seabird, washed ashore with the force of the gale.

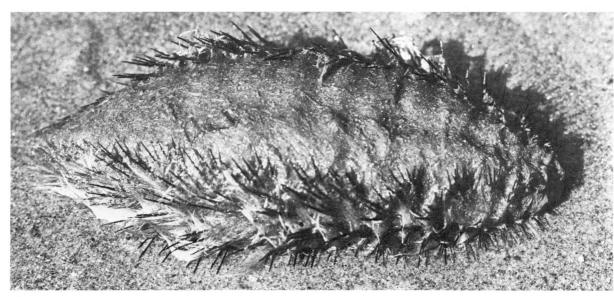

One unusual find was a cushion star, a species seldom found on the shore.

Right: Herring gull about to take off.

Below: Rarely found on the shore, this beautiful cushion star, would probably return to deeper water.

Far right: The angular crab.

November 4th

A still, quiet day with gulls resting on the gunwales of boats in the harbour. Mostly herring gulls and black-headed gulls.

    In the big pool I came across a crab which must have been washed in by the storm a little while ago. Called gonoplax it has enormous long claws and legs and its eyes are on long stalks which fit into perfectly matched grooves so that they can be protected in times of danger. I wonder how long before it returns to deeper water?

Prawns are still plentiful but anytime now they will move out into deeper and warmer water for the winter, an example of seasonal migration in the sea.

December 10th

A forest of sand mason worms has developed on the sandy part of the beach chiefly, I think, because there have been no people walking about and so destroying their tubes.

December 20th

Limpets. This is one shellfish that can always be found. They cannot move far and always return to the same spot where, in close

contact with the rock, they wait for the next feeding ramble. Some of these rather large limpets must be quite aged according to sea standards, perhaps as much as twenty years old. Proof of how strong is their attachment to the rock surface to be able to resist the power of all those storms there must have been through those years.

Above left: The tubes of the sand mason worm.

Below left: Common prawn. Small ones are to be found in most pools but larger ones live lower down the shore.

Below: The rock surface around these limpets has been browsed free of seaweeds, as they feed.

Chapter Seven

Winter storm

All the night long the great wind had blown out of the east, driving the sea into a mountainous seascape of giant waves that roared towards the beach. Each wave, acting like a giant bulldozer, scooped out tons of sand and mixed it into whirlpool currents that churned it all into a jumble of sand, stones and living creatures.

Next morning millions of shells were stranded in wide banks, some smashed by the force of the sea, others still alive but now facing a new threat. As the wind veered to the north the blizzard came and the shells on the surface of the heaps froze solid. Soon a covering of snow blanketed the beach.

By the morning of the second day the wind died away and the snow had melted and now the shells could be seen again.

Along the edge of the tide thousands of grey otter shells put out their syphons to breathe in the water that washed over them; razor shells tried to re-bury, whilst tellins, rayed trough shells and venus shells added their colours to the drab winter beach.

Then the gulls came. Herring gulls, common gulls, black-headed gulls, greater and lesser black-backs – the lot. Somehow the word was spread that food was here in plenty and soon the noisy rabble was eating more shellfish than they could ever remember.

Page 65: This stranded red-nose cockle is pushing out its long red foot in an effort to burrow down into the sand once more. Sometimes this foot is used to propel the shellfish back into the sea and to move about when it is living normally in the sand.

Above: Sometimes after a storm there are thousands of the white 'shells' or 'tests' of sea potatoes washed in. Most of them were probably killed by the large waves.

Bottom right: Otter shells stranded on the beach.

Top far right: Stranded rednose cockles.

Bottom far right: Sea mouse. A kind of marine worm that is sometimes stranded after a storm. Normally it would live in the muddy sand well out to sea. (Underside view.)

Normally a herring gull has to work hard to open a live shellfish. It flies up with the shell in its mouth and then releases it to fall on the hard sand or rocks. Eventually, after a number of attempts, the shell breaks and the gull can feed.

But today so many shells were broken and so many were killed by the bitter cold that the gulls were wading knee-deep in food, gorging without interruption.

One young herring gull seized a small wrasse which was frozen hard. A new experience and quite unlike the familiar soft fish it had eaten so often on the harbour quay. It turned it this way and that; it tried to swallow it head first but the stiff body wedged itself across its throat; it smashed it down after the manner of a thrush breaking a snail shell. The last I saw of it was it wandering off along the beach still gripping its useless prize. There was something a little pathetic in the way it clung to a fish it could not swallow, whilst surrounded by other easy pickings.

At the end of the beach were thousands of cockles lying in a bank some eighteen metres long by three metres wide. Their tough shells had preserved them from the gale and now a few were still alive and moving. Long red feet writhed in and out of the shells as they

sought their way back to the sea, the clicking of their shells sounding like tiny castanets playing a sorrowful tune for this sad, wasted, mass of dying shellfish.

Other forms of life had been affected by the storm. Sea mice (really large worms) littered the beach and their sides glowed where their rainbow-hued bristles caught the light. How strange that there should be so much beauty in an animal that spends its life buried beneath the black mud far out in the bay.

Masked crabs, green shore crabs, swimmers and many others seldom seen on the shore had taken cover under the heaped seaweed. These were the fortunate ones. All that was left of the others was an odd leg, an empty shell or a body with legs missing, a grim reminder of the violence of the storm.

Walking the strand line after such a gale is always exciting for you never know what may be stranded. Mermaid's purses, wood bored by teredo, goose barnacles and even the odd jellyfish swept up from warmer, southern seas. Nuts from other continents mix with the plastic rubbish from local places.

Today the tideline is becoming full of indestructible rubbish, plastic beakers, summer sandals, polythene bags and torn pieces of polythene sheeting, plastic trawl net and blocks of polystyrene. It is all so light that it avoids the grinding effect of sand and sea. What a pity we use the sea as a dump.

Then there is the oil. The black filth that uncaring ships' captains pump into the oceans. It spreads into a death-dealing film on the surface to choke and suffocate razor-bills, guillemots and gannets and finally drifts ashore to smother shiny,

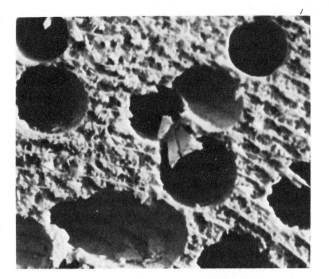

Top: When the tree is cut through it is found to be filled with holes.

Right: Drifted up on a piece of floating timber are these goose barnacles. A medieval myth told that these grew on trees and that from them grew barnacle geese.

68

colourful stones with its pall of stickiness.

We get the last of it – on the soles of our feet and on our clothes.

We can clean ourselves but for the seabirds there is no escape, only a slow dying on the merciless sea to be thrown ashore as a tattered oil-caked body that once flew free in the air and dived into the cool clear depths. An occasional oiled seabird survives long enough to stagger ashore, but by then it is too late for the oil will have done its work.

There was little oil after this gale and by the end of the week the sea was calm again. The empty shells had been collected by the souvenir makers, some of the shellfish had somehow returned to the sea and only heaps of seaweed told the story of the natural disaster which had played itself out on the beach.

On your beach

After a gale the best time to search a beach is when the waves die down in calmer weather because that is when many items are stranded. If you look along a beach you can usually see a rough sort of line where all manner of things have been left by the high tide. This is the strand line or tideline and is the best place to look.

On rocky shores you will often find drifted debris under large rocks.

If the seaweed is very thick upon the shore the chances are that many interesting things will be well mixed up with it so you may have to pull it apart. You can use a stick for this work.

Some floating items such as barrels and timber can be collected from the very edge of the foaming surf on a sandy beach, but watch out for the extra large wave which may sweep up a little farther and soak you.

Right: A common whelk and its egg capsules lie stranded. Each of the tiny capsules that go to make up the mass, contain up to twenty tiny whelks. Normally they are secure on the sea bed but the violence of the storm has thrown them ashore.

Make a collection of seashells

Collect any *dead* (not living) seashells. They should later be washed in a plastic bucket and then left to soak in water to which has been added a few ounces of household bleach. Next day they must be washed again and again until all trace of bleach disappears. Place them on newspaper to dry. Next they can be stuck on to thick, coloured cardboard or hardboard with a strong glue. Varnish with a clear varnish and label. Shoe boxes make good boxes to keep shells in.

Chapter Eight

Sandy shore

At first glance the beach looks as if it is lifeless. It looks to be a desert-like stretch of sand without foothold for animal or firm surface for seaweed holdfast. Yet living creatures are here in plenty, living out their lives in burrows a few centimetres under the surface. Over the years each has evolved its own method of surviving here among the moving sand grains.

Due to the small size of the grains on the surface they are always on the move, saturated with water but lacking the rich air supply that is found in the waves and open sea. A few centimetres deeper the sand is still most of the time.

So it is that many of the animals living here have long syphon tubes extending upwards to the surface and in this way a fresh supply of seawater can be taken down for breathing without the sand clogging everything up.

The lugworm is common on the beach and as many as six live in every square metre on the lower part of the shore. At first all you will see are the small round mounds like tiny volcanoes with a coiled worm of sand looking just as if it had been squeezed out of a toothpaste tube. This is called the cast. A few centimetres away will be a saucer-like depression known as the blow hole.

The lugworm lives in the bottom of a U-shaped burrow which is lined with mucus to prevent the sand falling into the shafts.

It burrows and feeds by eating its way through the sand which it draws down and takes out the edible pieces and then pushes the rest up to the surface where it forms the worm-like cast. Clean water for breathing and more sand and food are drawn down through the hollow hole nearby.

When the surf is breaking on the beach the bass swim in and feed on these worms which are often disturbed and thrown out of their burrows by the force of the waves.

I have stood on the beach in autumn when waves three metres high were hurling themselves down on to the sand and watched a fisherman angling for bass catch a six-pounder in that whirling maelstrom of rushing water.

How does a fish find food among so much water-flung sand and pebbles?

Another kind of worm living on the beach is the sand mason worm and this one builds its own tube, inside which it is safe from most

Left: This underside close-up of a sea potato plainly shows the paddle shaped spines that help it to burrow into the sand grains.

A lugworm. This one was dug up and placed between cast and blowhole so that you can see how big it is.

enemies. It makes this flexible tube of sand grains and small fragments of shells cemented together with a mucus which is given off from glands on the underside of its body. It simply mixes sand grains with the mucus and then takes them in its mouth and places them in the correct position. These tubes may be up to nearly a metre in length but the worm itself is only about twenty-five centimetres. It is a beautiful red worm with scarlet gills but very delicate and best left inside its tube.

Walking along the beach all one can see of the tube is the top few centimetres which stick up from the surface, the rest is buried below.

A vast number of shellfish live here in the sand, most of them in the top layer, no deeper than ten centimetres. Since they are protected by the surrounding sand they do not need strong shells like many of their relatives on the rocks. Most of the sandy shore shells are bivalves and their foot is used

Top right: Natica, the sea snail, with its huge foot extended as it would be when bulldozing through the sand.

Right: This close-up photograph of a sand mason worm tube shows how it is made up of small pieces of seashell and grains of sand.

Below: These mounds with their sandy 'worms' show that lugworms have burrows under the sand.

for burrowing quite unlike the foot of rocky shore shells which is used for attachment and crawling.

By far the prettiest are the thin tellins. About one and a half centimetres in length their shells are shaded from white through pink to deep red and mauve.

There's one patch of sand on the beach that is packed with banded wedge shells whose shells so resemble butterfly wings that some people call them butterfly shells.

Deep down lives the otter shell, a huge bivalve nearly fifteen centimetres across, but the record for deep burrowing goes to the razorfish which can go down nearly a metre in depth.

Whilst shell life is normally fairly safe from above, there are predators lurking below in the sand itself.

The most successful is natica, the sea snail. It has a huge foot, the front part of which curves up like a bulldozer blade, forcing the sand aside as the shellfish moves along.

As soon as it comes into contact with a wedge shell its foot spreads over and around it smothering it like a cloak. A small trickle of acid is then released on to the wedge shell and this begins to dissolve it. Eventually a hole about two millimetres across is bored through and then natica begins its meal, slowly eating the body of its victim.

The most common inhabitant here is the sea potato. It is a sea urchin but whereas the urchins living on rocky shores have strong rigid spines for wedging themselves into rock crevices, this one has paddle-shaped spines. These are used to dig down to a depth of some eight centimetres where it lives in a small burrow. To obtain a supply of clean seawater for breathing it pushes up a syphon

A sea potato lives under the sand and when it is exposed it quickly begins to burrow.

In a few minutes it has begun to disappear into the wet sand.

Soon it has almost completely disappeared below the surface.

tube the end of which rests on the sand surface.

Rarely are these urchins seen on the surface, but once or twice each year I find one and it is always dead, broken up by a herring gull. If you happen to be a sea potato the way to stay alive is to stay buried under the sand!

There are a host of signs to be read on the beach and many of these are the small depressions made by syphon tubes of buried shellfish.

Sometimes I find an extra large one, about dinner plate size, where a flounder or plaice had rested at high tide. Flatfish have a habit of swimming down to the sand and then flapping a great deal with their tail and fins to disturb the sand which rises in a sort of smoke-screen and then settles on their back, thus camouflaging them.

On the wet sand the tracks of birds do not last so long as those on the dunes, but there are feathers here which are signs of preening gulls and the odd broken shell that tells of a bird that has fed.

As the tide ebbs it often leaves its imprint in the form of gentle curving waves in the sand. They change in pattern each day and often in the hollows I find the empty back of a crab, a stranded hermit crab or the empty white 'shell' of a sea potato.

In summer, human footprints are everywhere, but in winter my own are often the only ones, to be erased later by the sea-wind.

On your beach

Make a collection of dead shells. Look for signs of life beneath your feet. With a small spade you could search for some of them.

If you find some tubes of tubeworms examine them with a hand lens.

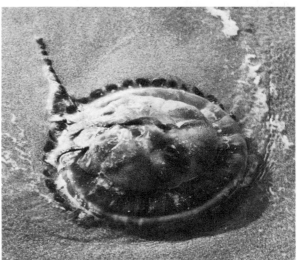

Top: Common starfish.

Below: A stranded jellyfish. Being nearly ninety-eight per cent water, a jellyfish very soon dies on the sand because it quickly begins to dry.

The male masked crab has very long pincer claws. This one is just beginning to burrow down again.

Chapter Nine

Night on a
summer shore

The fairy lights on the distant promenade send their multi-coloured reflections across the silent beach. The church clock in the tower of distant Stoke church chimed midnight as the whistling call of an oyster catcher broke out of the tide.

Night on the shore is an exciting time to go exploring and arriving at the beach I pumped hard on the pressure lamp, eager to start. A few sandhoppers attracted like moths to the sudden light, leaped up towards the flame, their hard bodies pattering on the metal bowl of the lamp.

After dark all the animals of the shore come out of hiding and move freely about their business, presumably because there is less chance of their being seen by predators like the herring gull.

In the rockpools the eyes of prawns glint as they swim and crabs of all sizes move with their curious sideways walk among the shadowy seaweeds.

I move quietly, being careful not to rattle the stones because I often find a blenny sitting out on a rock. Why they do this is a mystery, but I have seen them many times and one evening I watched one actually come out of the water. It used its pelvic fins as short legs and climbed up in the corner of a rockpool, settling down on the rock.

Blennies can breathe out of water for a while because a coating of slime covers their gills and oxygen can pass through this in much the same way as it does underwater.

Suddenly I saw one. Its large round eyes shone like tiny jewels and its clown-like lips gleamed white against the seaweed. But I had disturbed it and with a wriggle it slid into the water, the only sign that anything had happened being the ripples fading across the pool.

It's fun to walk at the edge of the tumbling waves as your lamp lights the water for there's an air of mystery as the restless sea rises and falls like a living thing and finally fades into blackness beyond the lamp's beam.

This particular night I thought I saw a

fisherman at the water's edge but my eyes in the poor light were playing tricks with my brain. As I drew nearer I saw it was a heron wading slowly away from me before rising on great spreading wings to fly across the moon and away.

Suddenly the sea exploded with a million silver sparks and I saw why the heron had been fishing there – a living stream of sand eels eddied to and fro, occasionally erupting into a cascade above the surface.

So many were there that the inshore edge of the vast shoal was moving like tinsel on to the beach. For several metres inshore the sand was alive with the movement of their bodies

for sand eels are equally at home wriggling through the sand or swimming free in the sea.

Perhaps this was a mating assembly, but whatever it was their numbers were out of this world. Maybe a million, maybe three million.

Taking off my waders I wandered in among them to stand in the silver stream of life and to feel their cold bodies surging around my legs. They stretched endlessly to right and left, beyond the rim of lamplight and out to where the sea grew darker in the depths.

After a while I moved on, my last sight of them was a wave, clogged with silver,

breaking fishily on the writhing shore.

By now it was nearly one in the morning. A razorfish stuck up out of the sand and I seized it, trying to tug it out and just a little surprised to feel the strength of its efforts to escape.

A second one, a third and then many more. By daylight I never see a single one but here under the moon they had come to the surface. I caught hold of another and pulled it out of the sand to lay it down and watch. Suddenly its long white foot sneaked out of one end of the shell, the tip searching for wet sand. It scratched at the surface making a small depression and then quickly pushed its way down. A pause. Then the foot went taut and the shell reared upwards as the muscles in the foot hauled on it, pulling it down into the sand.

In a series of eight to ten pulls the entire shell had disappeared and as it went back under the sand only a small oval depression told where it was.

I walked on. The beam of my lamp swung around to catch a masked crab burrowing away from the light. This one was a female with very short legs, but later I came across a big male busily pushing at the sand with its eight centimetre long nipper claws whilst its rear legs dug ever deeper. Slowly it disappeared leaving only the tube-like feelers stretching out from the sand.

In a shallow pool there was a pair of these crabs, the male using one pincer to hold on to the legs of the female to hold her above his head! He walked about in this manner, and since the female made no effort to escape I can only assume this was normal behaviour. Perhaps it was a form of courtship. However, I made a note to spend more time in the future studying the habits of these masked crabs.

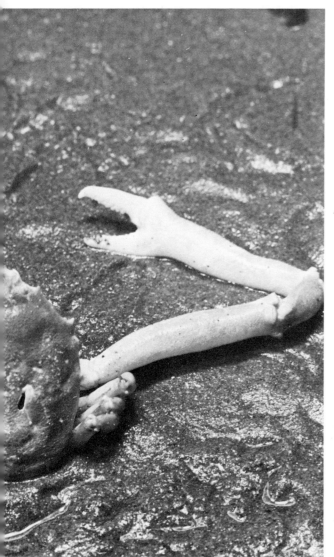

A pair of courting masked crabs photographed at night on the shore.

As I watched I was thinking how much there was to learn about even the humblest little animal, how many, many different aspects of their lives there was to watch.

I have a feeling that if I had all day, every day, for the rest of my life to study a single species there would still be so much to learn.

On another part of the beach I came upon a group of three burrowing starfish, which by the extent of their tracks had been very active on the surface. In the lamp's light, however, they set about burrowing, their tiny tube feet pushing aside the sand grains and thus allowing their bodies to sink deeper into the sand.

Unlike their relatives on the rocky shore, these starfish spend most of their lives tunnelling through the top few centimetres of the beach in search of food. It is a hungry predator and will catch and eat crabs, shellfish, worms and other starfish and urchins or even a sleepy fish. The prey is swallowed whole and any hard parts disgorged later.

I looked at my watch. Half past one and time to go. As I walked up the cliff path, a moth zoomed in on the lamp to fall in a fluttering heap on the dusty path. I shielded the light so that it should not be tempted once more to beam in to the hot glass, and very soon I was on the cliff top.

On your beach

Why not take your parents down to the shore one summer evening. Be sure to take a good powerful torch and make sure the tide is not coming in. Look in the rockpools. If you are fortunate you will see the phosphorescence on the waves.

Top: Three stages in the disappearance of a burrowing starfish.

Middle: Two minutes later.

Bottom: Once below the surface, the burrowing starfish sets off hunting through the sand for the small shellfish and crabs on which it feeds.

Far right: As dawn breaks a late hedgehog makes for the cover of marram grass. In a few minutes only its tracks will tell the story.

78

Chapter Ten

The dunes

Dawn came slowly, still and cool as the first rays of the sun reached out across the sea to touch the dunes. In the animal world it is the time when the creatures of the night seek their sleeping quarters and the daylight ones are barely waking. A black-headed gull, early risen, winged overhead, its feathers sighing sharply and then silence once more.

Half an hour later the sun was lighting a million drops of dew each suspended from the tip of a single marram grass spike. This capture of the dew is one way in which the dune plants get their moisture, for when the early breezes rustle through the marram the drops fall and return into the sand.

But I was here to read some of the messages left by the nocturnal wanderers. In the early morning tracks and signs are plain to see because the wind has not yet blown their edges away, and the low angle of the sunlight throws deep shadows which help to outline their shapes.

Here the sand was furrowed as if by tiny waves where wind-blown sand would soon be on the move again. Here, too, I found the first story. The footprints of a young rabbit as it loped along, then a fuzzy patch in the sand where it sat for a moment, perhaps to scratch. It had moved on under the side of a steep dune where sometime later a long-tailed field mouse had run across the rabbit's track. It

was obvious enough because the footprints of the mouse were right in the middle of one of the rabbit's paw marks. If the mouse had passed that way *before* the rabbit it is possible that the mouse's prints would have been destroyed at that point.

Reading prints is as simple as that. Just a little thought based upon the evidence in front of you. Let me give you another example that I saw later. A carrion crow had wandered along and strayed by chance on to the track of a natterjack toad. At that point the crow had changed direction and walked beside the toad tracks, perhaps hoping the toad was still near enough to provide a meal.

Above far left: Long-tailed field mice wander among the marram grass and live in burrows made into the damp sand where there is plenty of vegetation.

You can see that a rabbit passed this way quite early on because already the tracks have begun to erode as sand drifted by the wind fills them slowly in. Next came a hedgehog moving purposefully from left to right. Finally a natterjack toad came in from the right and crossed the hedgehog's tracks, circled around and then made off to the left. How do we know the hedgehog came along first? Simply because the tracks of the toad are superimposed upon them. The large footprints were made by myself investigating.

After a few yards the toad had walked into some undergrowth and at this spot the crow had flown off. Two deep footprints and the smallest impression of a wing tip told me this.

Walking over dunes is always exciting because there are so many things to find. A rabbit's skull bleached white, mussel and cockle shells with tell-tale signs showing they were carried there and opened by an oyster catcher, or a single feather of a curlew.

Half an hour later the wild and echoing alarm call of a redshank warned the life of the dunes that a stranger was among them. There was a pair of them and they had a nest with young among the saltings at the estuary edge.

I was now entering a part of the dunes where few people ever came, and here was a twisted pile of rusty barbed wire left over from the war. Now the wire served a new purpose. It held the nest of a carrion crow and as I drew near the young crouched low, hiding under the camouflage of their feathers that look so like the nest material itself.

In a slack – a wide open area where fine grasses had become established – an oyster catcher had a nest. A mere hollow with two well-camouflaged eggs. The mother bird had flown off as I came from behind a dune, so I took a quick look at the nest and noticed that the bottom of the small hollow was filled with dried rabbit droppings.

An unusual nest material you may think. But in fact the wind had simply blown the droppings along and some had come to rest in the small hollow of the nest.

At the very end of the dunes where they formed a narrow spit between the sea and estuary was a colony of black-headed gulls. Twenty thousand of them nest here and one has to be careful in walking for fear of stepping on a chick or unhatched egg.

Gulls everywhere. Gliding on the breeze, screaming at me and diving threateningly in an attempt to drive me off. Under every clump of marram grass a fledgling hid in the shadows.

Below left: Trail of a carrion crow. Perching birds tend to leave the toe mark at the rear. Carrion crows are common on sand dunes.

Below right: The tracks of an oyster catcher show where its beak has probed into the sand for sand hoppers. These little animals are very common on sandy beaches and can be found under seaweed on the tideline. They live in burrows a few centimetres deep and the oyster catchers know this and they search for them with their long beaks.

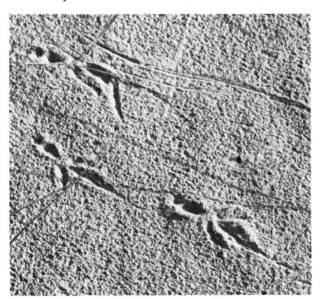

There are few places left in Britain where such sights can still be seen. For a few minutes I stood there, my ears filled with the sounds of this seabird city and my eyes full of wonder at the vast number of birds living there.

Black-headed gulls are beautiful in flight and I have often watched them quartering the beach, looking for odd scraps left by picnic parties.

These birds in this colony found most of their food in the town across the bay, living unnaturally off the rubbish dump, so in one sense human beings were directly responsible for the size of this colony.

A few herring gulls found the pickings easier here and had built their own nests at the edge of the colony. In this way they would seize black-headed chicks as food for their young.

Then it was time to walk on. Time to leave the birds to the wind, sea and sky as I turned to look for more signs.

At the top of the beach a few stray clumps of marram grew and around the base of these were the footprints of oyster catchers and every so often a hole in the sand where the beak had probed to seize one of the small sandhoppers that lived there.

Sandhoppers burrow into the sand to escape the heat and oyster catchers know this and so come here to feed. By night the hoppers crawl around leaving tiny tracks looking as if a thin chain had been laid on the sand.

It was time to return and in a little while I paused on the crest of a high dune. Behind me was the seabird city and the world of wildlife. In front a distant town with power boats moored in the estuary.

Already the first people were making their way to the summer beach, their footprints erasing those of the night creatures, yet few of them noticed the stories in the sand. For a little while I had shared the wild world of the other animals and learned a little more of their ways.

In the far distance the lonely call of a

Top: A natterjack toad on the dunes.

Above: Young black-headed gull chicks just out of the egg. The remains of the egg shell can be seen on the right. Another chick is just pipping its way out of the egg on the left.

Opposite top left: The eggs of an oyster catcher well camouflaged among coloured stones. The nest is a mere depression in the sand.

Opposite top right: Farther out on the dunes the occasional oyster catcher still nests. This one is covered with raindrops after a shower.

Right: A black-headed gull stands guard over its chick whilst waiting for the other parent to return with food.

curlew, contrasted with a motor horn, as the silence of the dunes gave way to the sounds of people and the town.

On your beach

Make some plaster casts of tracks. You will need some cardboard rings about five centimetres wide and about eighteen to twenty centimetres in diameter. You can make them by cutting across a detergent packet. Look around for a good plain and deep footprint and then surround it with your card ring and push it a little way into the sand. Mix up some plaster of Paris until it is like thin cream and pour this inside the ring until the track is covered by about three centimetres of plaster. Leave for twenty minutes to harden, then lift. Wash it off under a tap at home and leave to dry. A collection can be made and each one painted if you so wish.

You can make drawings of tracks too.

Right: Eider duck nesting on dunes well hidden among marram grass.

Below: A sandhopper coming out of its burrow.

Far right: A friendly herring gull sits and waits for food.

Chapter Eleven

The old fisherman

One other person regularly shares the beach with me and he's an old fisherman who has known it far longer than I. He is called Len and five years ago he set his seine net for the last time on this beach. Before that he fished the bay every summer and autumn.

He would load the net carefully into his dinghy, pulling it on to the top of a piece of canvas laid across the stern and this had to be done with great care because soon he would be shooting his seine around a shoal of fish.

The net was rather like a long, deep tennis net and was made so that along its top edge was a series of corks which buoyed it up and attached to its bottom line was a series of lead weights which stretched it downwards thus making a long wall of net in the sea.

When the seine was all set in place, Len would row around to the beach. His nephew usually came along and this young lad would leap ashore with the ropes and leave them piled on the sand. One rope was attached to the top of the net and the other to the bottom.

Back in the boat again the boy would begin to throw out the net as Len rowed out to sea and then around in a large horseshoe shape, returning to the shore a hundred yards farther along. This made a sort of wall as I already explained and due to Len's skill as a

fisherman he usually knew when a shoal was about and his aim was to entrap them within his seine net.

Once ashore they began to haul in and since it was quite heavy going they were always glad of a little help so those of us who were on the beach would divide up and take each end. Slowly the circle of floating corks would come closer in and slowly the two ends were brought together by the groups of men walking towards each other.

As the corks came ever closer you could feel a growing excitement. Len, in particular, would keep his eyes fixed on the quiet area of water within the bobbing corks for this is

gleaming, flashing catch of mackerel were brought out on to the sand.

Sometimes of course the net was empty. At other times if the catch was mullet, the fish would break out over the top of the net and as soon as one or two fish succeeded in doing this, the whole shoal would follow.

But all this was five years ago and now Len finds that all the heavy work that goes with seine net fishing is a bit too much for him. So the net hangs in his boat store smelling of tar, creosote and dried seaweed and sadly in need of repair.

Seining on the beach was a way of life that has no place in today's world. Marketing

where the first fish might break surface.

Closer and still no movement of fish.

Suddenly the sea would erupt into boiling foam as the mackerel shoal sensing danger and finding no escape underwater leaped for freedom. But very few succeeded in jumping the rope held by the corks.

Then the last few feet of net would come ashore as Len and I would rush into the water and hold the net high in our hands as the the fish brings too little profit and the many

Above: The seine net is hauled in.

Left: Netting, store pots for crabs, fish baskets, marker buoys, ropes, canvas covers for boats and crabbing boats on the beach.

power boats that tow the water skiers tend to break up the shoals and drive them out from the shallow waters where such nets can be used.

Len still fishes a moored net. This too is rather like the tennis net idea and he attaches one end to the pier whilst the other end is fixed to an anchored buoy.

The net hangs in the tide and at night herring swim into it and get their gills caught in the meshes. Next morning at dawn Len rows out and hauls up the net, sometimes to take two or three stone of herring but more often to return with a dozen or so fish that are not enough for the fishmonger but a good meal for his large family.

He also works a line of crab pots which he puts down just outside the seaward end of rollers reef.

He knows every gully and crevice where lobsters lurk and that's pretty clever when you think about it because he's never been down there to look around. He has learned it all by remembering where he has caught them in the past and he knows that once a lobster has been caught and its hole is deserted it will not be long before another home seeker takes over.

By memorizing the spot and by taking bearings from objects on the land he is able to row to exactly the same spot another time.

Fishermen carry a kind of detailed chart of their favourite fishing grounds in their memories. The chart has never been drawn but its outlines are passed from father to son by word of mouth as they fish together. Good spots are jealously guarded and given names like 'The Hole', 'Eastern Gut' and 'The Ridge'.

Len makes his own lobster pots. Every March he cuts some young willow shoots from a small plot of land known as the stool beds where the willows grow in rows like any other crop. For the rest of the year the place is undisturbed and the haunt of duck, heron and dabchick.

Back at his boathouse he weaves his pots by twisting the shiny golden-green shoots into an intricate pattern, until the pot is completed. Later in the year he will fasten rocks from the beach inside to weigh them down and hold them steady on the seabed.

Making willow pots is a dying craft and today many fishermen prefer to use pots made from plastic tubing which apparently last very much longer.

Len catches all sorts of creatures in his pots, from lobsters to spider crabs and hermit crabs to sea urchins. In some summers when the sea warms up more than usual, octopus occasionally get hauled up. These animals go into the pots after the crabs for these are their staple food.

The octopus which I have seen in the bay

are fairly small, about sixty centimetres from tentacle tip to tentacle tip. The largest one I have ever seen had a body the size of a rugger ball, arms as thick as mine and a metre long with suckers the size of a five pence piece.

Octopus in our waters are fairly harmless creatures, being very much afraid of human beings and keeping well out of our way. But Len doesn't like them because they eat the crabs and lobsters he is after and I guess that is fair enough.

Len has a hobby. A few times each year he goes down to the beach to spear razorfish, or oddfish as he calls them. He has made a one metre long spear from some four millimetre gauge wire. The end which he heated in his fire was beaten and filed into the shape of a narrow spear point.

Holding this in his right hand he walks *backwards* along the beach. The reason for this strange behaviour is that the pressure of his feet disturbs the razorfish who immediately begin to burrow and in so doing send up a jet of water out of the sand. This gives Len their position. If he walked

Above left: The old fisherman probes with his spear for razorfish.

Below left: An hour later his fishing bag is filled and a few extra razorfish lie beside it.

Below: Whelk pots on the quay.

forwards the jet would be behind him and he would not see it, so he walks backwards.

As soon as he sees the jet of water he pushes the end of the spear into the burrow. Gently he turns it this way and that, probing all the while a little deeper. Len has those sensitive hands that can tell the feel of the razorfish from all the small stones and pieces of shell that abound here.

Down . . . down . . . down goes the spear. Then a pause, and up it comes with a razorfish on the end. The action is repeated again and again for the next hour until he has gathered well over a hundred in the old tattered canvas bag.

Len eats them, and sometimes I try my luck with a spear he has made for me, but I'm no good at it. If I get six I reckon I am doing very well, but Len usually gives me a couple of dozen so at least my appetite is satisfied, if not my honour.

As Len grows older he spends less and less time spearing his oddfish, catching herring and making crab pots, but most days when the sun is out he's somewhere around leaning on the sea wall and looking out to sea – or more likely, he'll be swapping fisherman's tales with some of his cronies.

On your beach
If there is a fishing harbour nearby go along and look at the various kinds of net and fish-catching devices you can find in such places.

Have you ever looked really closely at the meshes of a net or the way in which a crab pot is made?

If there are a number of boats in the harbour you may begin to notice that each is built in a particular way to carry out the particular fishing job for which it was designed.

If people collect shellfish near your home why not go along and watch how they do it?

Watch fishermen repairing their nets.

Make lists of the names of the fishing boats and also their port of registration number and letters.

Chapter Twelve

Watcher on the
shore

The cormorant had been fishing for the past half an hour with no luck at all. It paddled slowly along, pushing its head beneath the surface again and again before diving: then it was ten seconds, twenty seconds and a few more out of sight before it bobbed up again – each time without a fish.

Then, after a particularly long dive, it came up with a flounder held across its beak.

First it turned the fish towards its gullet and stretching its neck upwards it jerked away in an effort to swallow the fish, but alas it was too large.

During the next ten minutes it tried again and again and once or twice it even cracked the fish down on to the sea's surface but whatever it did had no effect. The fish could not be swallowed.

Suddenly a great black-backed gull dive-bombed the cormorant, its hooked beak slashing at the fish. By the time the spray had settled the cormorant had dived with the flounder still in its beak.

A cormorant having landed on the branch of the old tree looks around to make sure everything is safe.

Preening is most important to a bird. Let's begin with a scratch. Ah, that's better.

Left: Next a little rubbing of the throat against the tail feathers . . . and that's not as easy as it looks.

Below: The angle of the wings is altered so that every feather gets its share of sun and wind.

The black-backed gull floated on the still sea obviously waiting for the cormorant to reappear, which it did fairly soon. Immediately the gull attacked and equally quickly the cormorant dived again.

This time the gull swam swiftly, holding its head to one side and looking downwards, obviously watching the underwater swimmer below.

This time when the cormorant broke surface the gull was right there, but once more the black fisherman disappeared below. This action was repeated several times.

Then the cormorant surfaced *without* the flounder.

I watched it as it circled slowly until the gull decided that its free meal had disappeared and it flew off beyond the headland. For a while the cormorant continued to swim in a tight circle, warily searching the sky for its enemy. At last it dived and quickly surfaced with the flounder in its beak.

I am quite sure the cormorant had outwitted its enemy by leaving the fish on the seabed, knowing it to be dead.

It apparently also remembered it could not swallow its prey for it soon took to the air still holding the flounder. As it flew away towards Cod Rocks I hoped it would enjoy the meal it had so cleverly guarded.

I remember another time and another black-backed gull, and this at dawn when the sea was mirror calm. The gull was gliding in towards the shore when it suddenly braked and crashed into the water, its head and half its body going under in a flurry of spray.

As the spray cleared I could see the gull was trying to take off, its great wings beating the air and its webbed feet thrusting at the sea surface whilst its head every so often was pulled under. With tremendous effort it began to rise, dragging from the depths a cuttlefish which, as soon as it entered the air, sent a jet of black ink across the breast of the gull.

It was a last defensive gesture, for the gull landed on the beach to deliver one or two hammer blows on its prey before beginning its meal.

Then on another day there was the old grey seal. I had been sitting on a rock chatting to an angler who had been fishing without luck. He had been at it most of the day and his bag was still empty.

Suddenly the sea within a few feet of us erupted and a sleek head thrust up, holding a two-pound bass in its be-whiskered mouth. Its two limpid eyes regarded us as if to say 'Well I thought I'd just show you how we professionals do it!' Then it was gone.

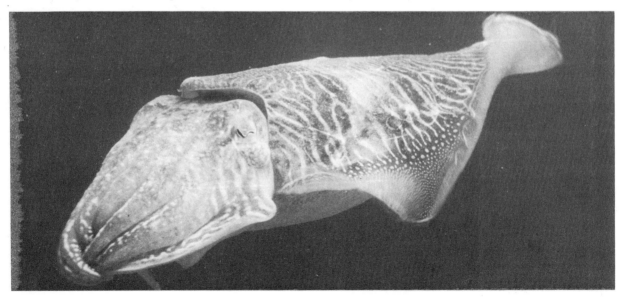

A different kind of fisherman is the basking shark. These huge harmless sharks come inshore in May and swim slowly up and down along the bay.

I once sailed alongside one of these ten metre monsters and was able to look down as it swam less than a metre below the surface. Its vast mouth was open like a cellar door as it sieved through the sea catching the plankton on which it fed.

How strange that the largest fish that comes into the beach feeds only on the smallest of living creatures.

I sailed beside this one quite slowly and for a brief moment we gazed into each others eyes, I with admiration for a magnificent animal, and the shark perhaps merely aware of the white outline of my boat.

I have a great regard for basking sharks and well remember one hot day in May when some unknown excitement seized them. One by one or sometimes six together they leaped out of the waves to crash back with a sound like thunder sending a smother of spray eight metres into the air.

I know not why they did it and can only report that it was a magnificent sight, as thrilling as anything I have ever seen.

Then one late September an otter came out of the sea and trotted across the reef before slipping silently out of sight, no doubt to search the laminaria beds for a pollack or mullet. Perhaps it returned to the estuary at nightfall.

One day the harbourmaster telephoned. He was receiving reports of strange swimming objects coming up to the surface around some of the moored yachts. He said there was a large number of them and they looked like peanuts in size but were darker in colour. I was most intrigued by his description and set off for the harbour with a bucket and net.

He was waiting for me with a small dinghy and soon we were rowing out to search. Suddenly he pointed to where a rippling ring of water disturbed the otherwise calm surface of the harbour.

I made a sweep with the net – and missed whatever had made the small swirl. Then another and another. This time the net came in with the mystery object. It was a small shellfish called the lobe shell or helmet bubble shell.

This shell normally lives on the seabed, crawling through the muddy sand in sheltered places such as harbours and inlets, but once or twice each year it takes to swimming. For some unknown reason large numbers of them begin to swim at the same time and the movement is quite extraordinary.

What strange impulse brought this about? Why had they left the muddy darkness to swim into the sunlit upper waters among the keels of holiday craft?

I do not know the answer and perhaps I never will discover it. One day a marine biologist will study this tiny shellfish and perhaps discover some of the answers about its way of life and then he will write up the results of his work so that the information is available for all people who wish to learn.

Far left and left: Cuttlefish. The living cuttlefish is an extraordinary animal which is jet propelled when moving fast, but which uses its fins to move quietly and slowly. It has two long prehensile arms beneath its head and these are armed with suckers. It shoots them out to catch shrimps and small fish.

For my part I was excited by what I saw, for they were quite beautiful.

Like so many stories that begin on the beach, the end is not always written there and to complete the story may take many years of searching and patient discovery.

But one thing is certain. There are stories beginning every moment of the day and all we need is a little time to watch the ever-changing life of the creatures and plants that live here on the beach.

Beyond the beach, stretching into the distance over the horizon lies the sea. It covers two-thirds of our world's surface and because of its immensity we regard it as a vast reserve of life. For millions of years it has been there and slowly a rich variety of life has evolved in its waters.

But today there is hardly a square mile of ocean that does not bear the burden of pollution.

Unthinkingly we use the sea as a dump for Man's unwanted, industrial waste and throughout the waters of the world drift microscopic droplets of waste oil and chemicals.

The sea is approaching a condition wherein the life it supports will find survival increasingly difficult. As you grow older would you rather enjoy clear oceans, clean beaches and bright birds calling . . . or murky seas with oiled seabirds creeping on to filthy beaches?

The choice is yours.

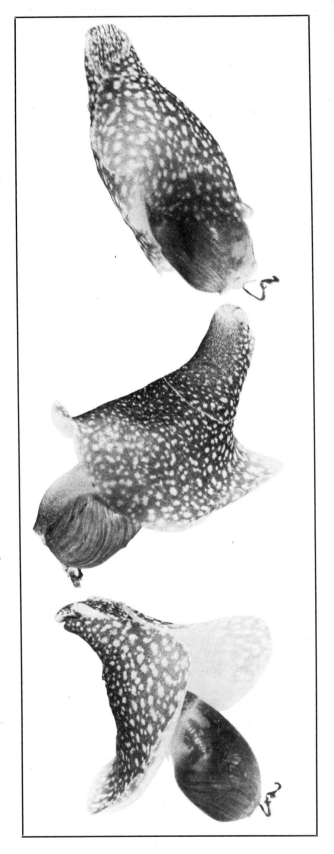

Top: A lobe or helmet bubble shell leaps from the mud in which it has been crawling . . .

Middle: . . . and lifts into the upper waters. . . .

Bottom: Eventually the shell rises into the sunlit upper waters. It swims there for a while . . . and then returns to the depths, and the mud.

94

Index